The Classic
Piano *Course*

The complete course for older beginners

CAROL BARRATT

This book comes with a complimentary dummy keyboard.

T0057733

Cover design by Pearce Marchbank
Cover illustration by Brian Grimwood
Music processed by New Notations

Order No. AM 981277
International Standard Book Number: 0.8256.3325.7

Music Sales America

DISTRIBUTED BY

HAL•LEONARD®
CORPORATION

7777 W. BLUEMOUND RD. P.O. BOX 13819 MILWAUKEE, WI 53213

Preface

A big "thank you" to Naomi Saxl for her integrity and her editorial support.

A big "well done" to Christine Hawker who couldn't play the piano and who now can!

Pictures in this book are reproduced by permission of
the Royal College of Music, the Holton Deutsch Collection Limited, and the Mary Evans Picture Library,
and are credited in captions under each picture.

CONTENTS

General Topics

Pieces

Introducing the Keyboard

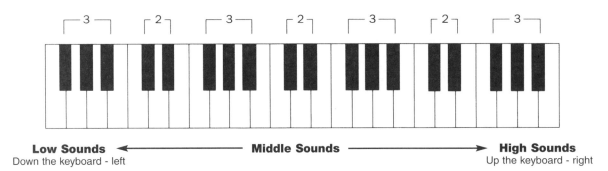

Low Sounds ⟵   **Middle Sounds** ⟶ **High Sounds**

Down the keyboard - left   Up the keyboard - right

The piano keyboard has white keys and black keys, with the black keys in groups of twos and threes. Starting with the lowest, find all the groups of two black keys on the piano.

Middle C

The note **C** is the white key to the left of the two black keys to the middle of the keyboard is called **Middle C.**

and the **C** that is closest

The Musical Alphabet

There are only seven letters used in music and they are the first seven letters of the alphabet - **A B C D E F G.** These same letters are used over and over again. The distance from one note to the next note with the same letter-name is called an **Octave.**

The White Keys

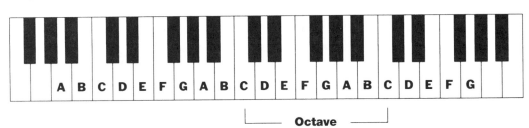

Practice finding all the **C**s on the keyboard, then all the **G**s.

With your right hand choose a group of three high black notes and play the **A** nearby.

With your left hand choose a group of two low black notes and play the **D** nearby.

What are the notes marked with a **✱**?

Introducing notation

Notes show the player which keys to play on the piano and are written on the five lines and four spaces which comprise the **staff.**

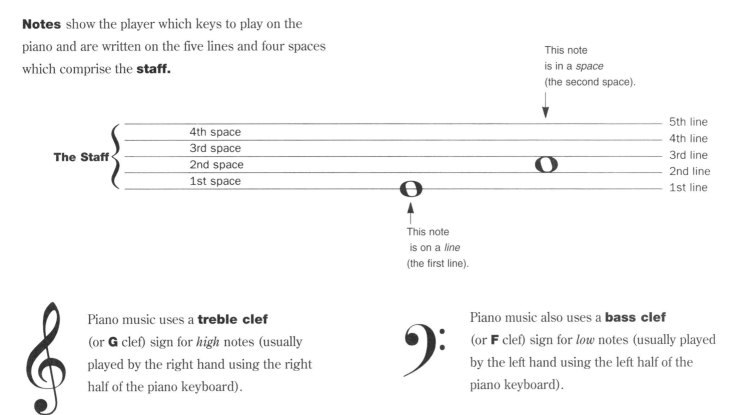

Piano music uses a **treble clef** (or **G** clef) sign for *high* notes (usually played by the right hand using the right half of the piano keyboard).

Piano music also uses a **bass clef** (or **F** clef) sign for *low* notes (usually played by the left hand using the left half of the piano keyboard).

For piano music, two staves are joined together by a **brace** - one staff for each hand - and this is called the **grand staff.**

Middle C

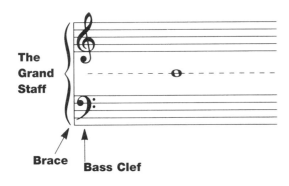

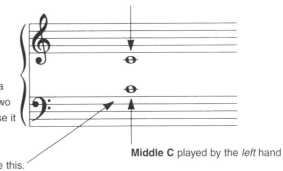

Music is divided into **measures** or **bars** with vertical **barlines.** At the end of a piece of music is a *double* barline.

Each measure contains a number of **beats.**

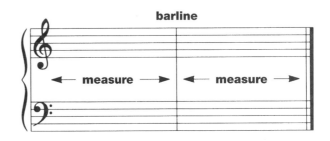

Introducing time

Each piece of music has various patterns of *long* and *short* notes. These patterns are called **rhythm.**

The *position* of the note on the lines and spaces of the staff tells you which key to play, but it is the *shape* or design of the note that tells you its time value; i.e., its length in terms of rhythm.

Note Values

There are different types of notes for different lengths of notes (beats).

whole note	𝅝	has **4 beats**	**1 - 2 - 3 - 4**
dotted half note	𝅗𝅥.	has **3 beats**	**1 - 2 - 3**
half note	𝅗𝅥	has **2 beats**	**1 - 2**
quarter note	𝅘𝅥	has **1 beat**	**1**

Time Signature

The **time signature** is written at the beginning of a piece of music to indicate the number of beats in each measure. Note values add up in each measure to make this time signature.

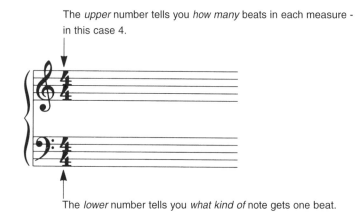

The *upper* number tells you *how many* beats in each measure - in this case 4.

The *lower* number tells you *what kind of* note gets one beat.

4 = 𝅘𝅥 (a quarter of a whole note). Therefore, in the time signature of ⁴⁄₄ there are 4 beats in each measure and each beat is a 𝅘𝅥

Right Time!

Place the thumb of your right hand on **Middle C** and play this as you count the following rhythm:

Count   1 - 2 - 3 - 4   1 - 2 - 3 - 4   1 - 2 - 3 - 4   1 - 2 - 3 - 4

How to sit at the piano

Posture

It is important to sit correctly at the piano; otherwise, you may develop back problems. Sit facing the middle of the keyboard, making sure that you are sitting straight but relaxed. If you feel uncomfortable, lean slightly forward. Adjust your piano stool so that your arms are an inch or so above the keyboard. Make sure your feet are flat on the floor - the right foot may be slightly forward.

Hand Position

Correct hand position

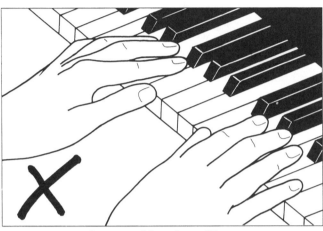

Incorrect hand position

Curve the fingers so that the top of the finger plays the key by falling directly from above. Imagine you are holding a small object in the hollow of your hand as you play and keep your wrist in line with your arm. Place the thumb tip near the tip of the forefinger to form a sort of 0. Keep your nails short!

Don't play with flat fingers - if you do, your hand will not be flexible and you will never be able to play anything fast or expressively. Although the fingers should be directly above the keys, make sure that you touch only the key that is being played. Try not to look at your hands as you play.

Fingering

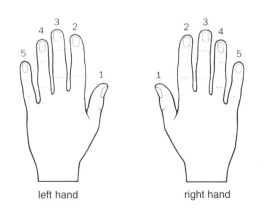

left hand   right hand

> **Fascinating snippet**
> Two piano teachers advocating 'the peaceful wrist' movement: Clementi used to place coins on his pupils' wrist and Moscheles wanted his pupils to play passages of music with glasses of water balanced on their wrists! These ideas seem rather extreme, don't try them out, but bear them in mind.

To make learning easier, the fingers of both hands are given numbers. Fingering is numbered from the thumb, this being number 1.

Practice moving each finger as you say its number aloud.

Muzio Clementi (1752-1832)

Ready to play

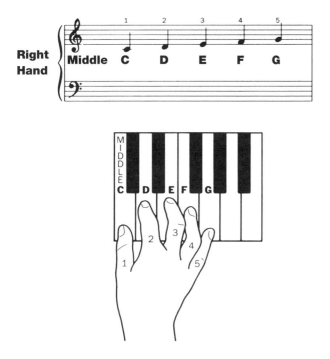

Right Hand

Middle C D E F G

Place your right hand in the position shown.
You are now ready to play the notes **C D E F G.**
Play these five notes going up and then down.
Look at where the notes are positioned on the staff;
i.e., on which line or space.

Legato

As you play the exercises below, hold each note
until you play the next note, then let it go - it is a "see-saw"
action. This kind of touch is called *legato* - Italian for smooth
or "joined-up." It is used for most of the music you will play.
Think of smooth, even, connected—but make sure that one
sound does not overlap with the next.

Starting points - *Right hand*

Look at the time signature of each exercise and count evenly as you play.

1.

2.

Now practice the above exercises saying the letter-names
(in time) as you play. Notice where each note is written
on the staff: **D** is in the space *below* the staff, **E** is *on*
the first line, and **F** is *in* the first space.

Au Clair de la Lune

Repeated notes can't be played with a *true* legato. In measure 1, try to play the three repeated **C**s as smoothly as you can - the following notes, **C** to **D** to **E** etc., are easily played legato.

:|| = Repeat sign - repeat from the beginning or from the nearest ||:

Accompaniment for teacher (or friend, son, or daughter!)

Shoo Shaggie

(Counts are not usually written in - you should always count in your head.)

Teacher's accompaniment

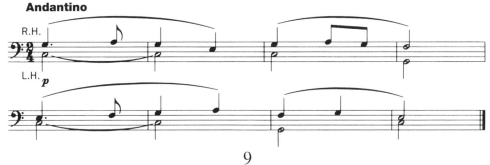

Change hands

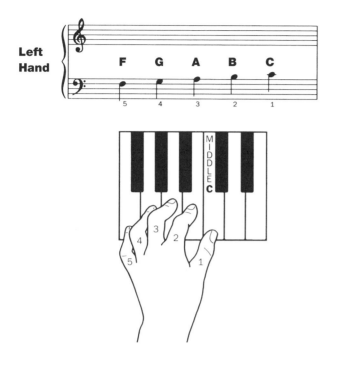

Left Hand

Place your **left hand** in the position shown.

You are now ready to play the notes **F G A B C.**

Play these five notes going down from **Middle C** and then up. Notice where each note is positioned.

Look at page 12: the *stems go up* on the *right* of the note head from **Middle C** upwards.

On this page: on these notes the *stems go down* on the *left* of the note head from **Middle C** downwards.

Hints and Reminders

1. Listen as you play - make sure that you are playing legato.
2. Try not to look down at your hands.
3. Remember to hold your fingers in a curved shape.

Starting points - *Left hand*

Now practice the above exercises saying the letter-names (in time) as you play. Notice where each note is on the staff: **B** is *in* the space *above* the staff, **A** is *on* the fifth line, **G** is *in* the fourth space.

Air des Bouffons

f = *forte* = loud p = *piano* = soft

When you play a key with a little weight or pressure, you make a *soft* tone.

When you use more weight, you make a *loud* tone.

French Folk Tune

Teacher's accompaniment

Largo
from the *"New World" Symphony*

Adapted from
Antonin Dvořák (1841–1904)

Slowly

Teacher's accompaniment

Slowly

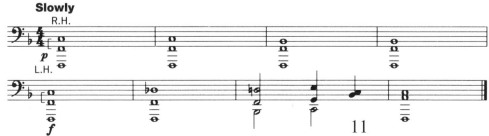

Suggested listening

Slow movement from this *Symphony in E minor.* The tune above is played by the Cor Anglais, which gives a tranquil quality to the melody. (You will notice that the rhythm in this version is much simpler than the original.)

11

Pick 'n' Mix
A multi-piano workout

These four exercises will work *together* - at the same time.

If you are on your own, just practice each exercise separately. You could record one or two of them to play alongside.

If you are in a group situation with two or more keyboards, put each exercise at a comfortable octave for each player - higher or lower.

Two or three players at one piano can be quite an experience!

Exercise 1 should be played at the highest pitch and the 𝄢 exercises must be positioned below the 𝄞 exercises.

Experiment with the different areas of the keyboard.

1.   C.B.

2.   C.B.

Teacher's accompaniment

This must be played *above* all the other parts. Play it one or two octaves higher than written.

Suggested listening

This "workout" is written in "waltz" time. Listen to *The Blue Danube Waltz* by Johann Strauss II (1825–1899) to put you in the mood. You will be playing an excerpt yourself before you reach the end of this book.

Alternating hands

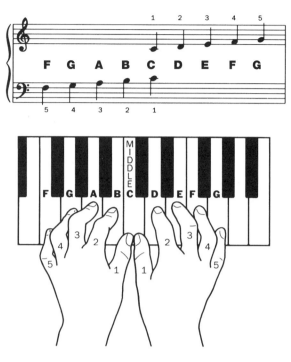

Place **both hands** in the position shown.

Play these nine notes in contrary motion (both hands moving together but in different directions; e.g., from fingers 1–5 and back) starting from both thumbs on **Middle C.**

The following pieces will contain notes in both the treble **and** bass staves.

Reading Hint

When notes move from space to space or line to line, skip one white key.

E to **G**
skip **F**

G to **B**
skip **A**

Accent

>(♩ 𝅘𝅥) = *Accent* (play slightly louder than other notes).

Hint: Decide how loud or soft you want a key to sound *before* you play it.

A Surprise!
Theme from the *'Surprise' Symphony*

Adapted from
Joseph Haydn (1732–1809)

> **Fascinating snippet**
>
> The *'Surprise' Symphony* is so-called because of the sudden loud chord that bursts into the slow movement of which Haydn had said, "That will make the ladies jump." In this adaptation you have only one loud note; in the symphony, the chord played by the orchestra is reinforced by a loud drum sound.

14

Canons

A canon is a piece of music where two or more parts follow each other with the same tune.

When you reach *, a teacher or friend can join in, starting from the beginning, to make a proper canon. If you are in a group lesson, other pupils can join in at other octaves or on other pianos.

Tallis's Canon

Pieces don't always start on the first beat of the measure. In this piece, the last measure has only three beats because the first bar *began* on beat 4. (First and last measures must add up to the time signature.)

Count **123** and then start playing on **4.**

Thomas Tallis (1505–1585)

Teachers start on

Fascinating snippet
Tallis's Canon was written during the reign of Queen Elizabeth I. Later, Benjamin Britten (1913–1976) used it in his opera *Noye's Fludde.*

Barratt's Canon!

C.B.

Teachers start on

15

Rests

Rests represent a period of silence in a piece of music. Each note value has its own rest sign. For example, a silence lasting as long as a quarter note is shown by a quarter rest ₹.

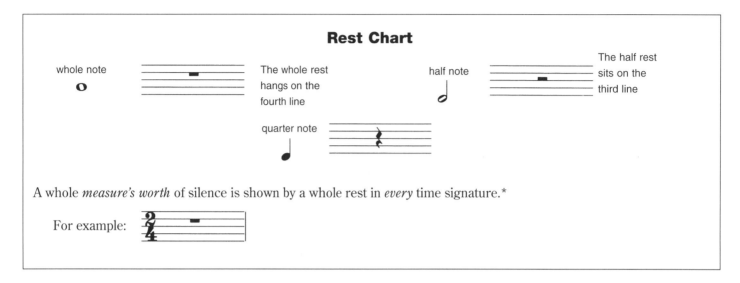

A whole *measure's worth* of silence is shown by a whole rest in *every* time signature.*

For example:

Rest Exercise

Lift your hand off the key when you see a rest sign - don't hang on when you should be resting!

(The rest counts are given in parentheses in the following exercise.)

From this point on, exercises using one hand will use one staff only.

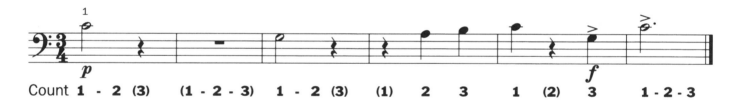

Count **1 - 2 (3)**   **(1 - 2 - 3)**   **1 - 2 (3)**   **(1)**   **2**   **3**   **1**   **(2)**   **3**   **1 - 2 - 3**

(Resting!) On the Bridge at Avignon

French Folk Song

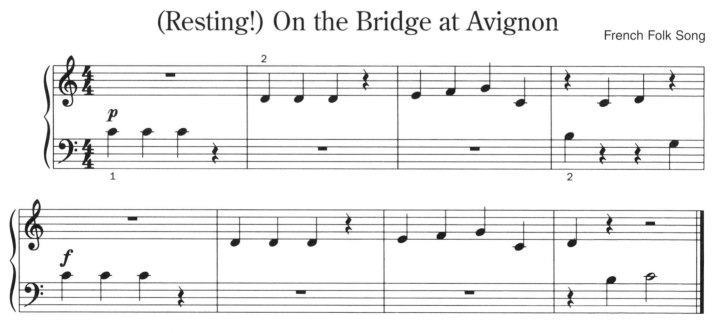

* except in $\frac{4}{2}$ and $\frac{8}{4}$

Tied notes

A **tie** (⌣ or ⌢) is a small curved line joining two notes on the *same* line or space.

The relevant piano key is then held down for the total value of *both* notes.

1 - 2 - 3 - 4 - 1 - 2 - 3 (4)

Ties are mostly used when notes last across a barline.

Play the first note of a tied note and then hold on and count the second note.

count   1   2   3 - 1 - 2   3

When the Saints Go Marching In

Try tapping out the rhythm written as ↓ .

Now tap this rhythm on your left leg with your left hand as you play the tune with your right hand - good for developing coordination.

If you find this too difficult at first, practice tapping out the rhythm of *both* parts together, one on each leg.

(If you are in a group situation, other pupils could clap or tap the given rhythms or invent different rhythms.)

Traditional American Song

> **Fascinating snippet**
> This tune was often played by Dixieland Jazz musicians at funerals in
> New Orleans. It was originally a Negro spiritual.

17

New position

Place your **left hand** in the position shown.

You are now ready to play the notes **C D E F G** an octave below **Middle C.**

Play these five notes going up and down from the new C.

Stems

Above the third line the stems go *down*.

Below the third line the stems go *up*.

On the third line the stem can go *up* or *down*.

Ode to Joy
Theme from the last movement of the *Ninth Symphony*

Fascinating snippet

This symphony has more than stood the test of time; it is one of the greatest masterpieces ever written, despite the composer's worsening deafness. However, when it was first performed, not all critics were complimentary: "We find Beethoven's *Ninth Symphony* to be precisely one hour and five minutes long; a fearful period indeed, which puts the muscles and lungs of the band, and the patience of the audience to a severe trial…. The last movement, a chorus, is heterogeneous. What relation it bears to the symphony we could not make out…." (*The Harmonicon*, London, April 1825.)

Adapted from
Ludwig van Beethoven (1770–1827)

continued
on
next
page

*Your ear may want your finger to play this more correct but more difficult rhythm. See page 21.

Eighth Notes

An **eighth note** ♪ (or ♪) is twice as fast as a quarter note: ♩ = ♪ + ♪

Two eighth-notes are usually joined together to make one beat: ♩ = ♫

To start with, say the word "and" between the beats.

Emphasize the main beats, keeping the "ands" softer.

count as
you play

1   +   2   3   +   1-2-3
          (and)

𝄾   ♪ rest

Phrase marks

The long curved lines over the notes below are called **phrase marks.**

Music, like language, is expressed in phrases. A *phrase* is a musical sentence or idea - imagine taking a breath at the end of each phrase mark and lift your hand off briefly without changing speed.

Unless directed otherwise, play all the notes within each phrase mark smoothly (legato).

Add two phrase marks to "Ode to Joy" on page 18.

Ode to Joy
(continued from previous page)

Count   1   2   3   4   1   2   +   3   4   1   2   +   3   4   1   2   3 - 4

*(♩.   ♪ ♩)

Now play all sixteen bars of the "Ode to Joy" theme continuously.

Suggested listening
Beethoven's *Ninth Symphony* (last movement) and Brahms'
First Symphony (see page 22) (last movement). This symphony
by Brahms is often referred to as "Beethoven's Tenth"!

Din, Don

Spanish Folk Song

Teacher's accompaniment

Shepherd's Hey

In a measure of ⁴⁄₄ if the *first* or *last* two beats are eighth notes, they can be grouped in fours.

English Country Dance

Suggested listening
Percy Grainger's folk dance arrangements make interesting listening.

Dotted quarter notes

A dot placed after a note makes it half as long again.

A *dotted quarter note* ♩. = ♩ ♪   ♩. ♪♩ = ♩ ♫♩

Clap the rhythm for measures 1 through 4 of the "Skye Boat Song."

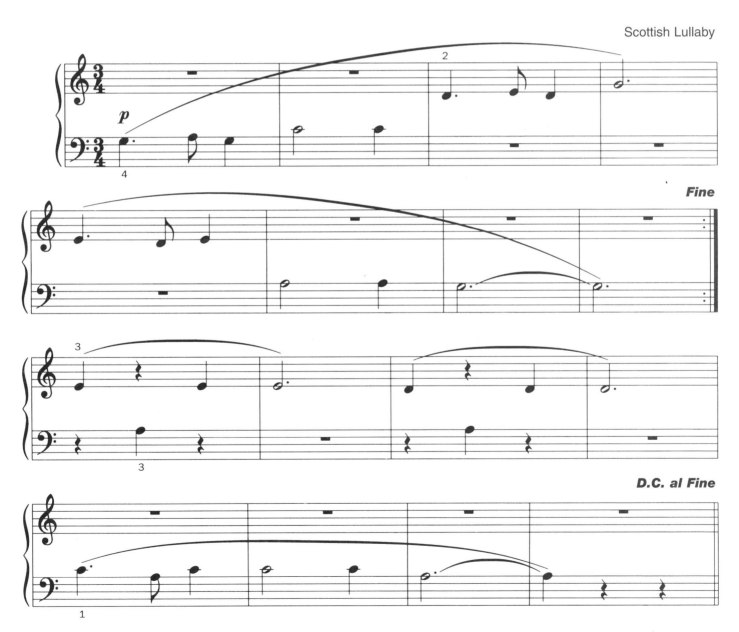

Skye Boat Song
A Lullaby from the Isle of Skye

D.C. *(Da Capo)* = repeat from the beginning.

D.C. al Fine = back to the beginning and finish at the word **Fine.**

21

Flats

The distance between any note and the very next note up or down is called a half step.

A **flat** sign (♭) makes a note a half step *lower* (to the left on the keyboard);

e.g., **B**♭ is the black key just below **B.**

Hint: When approaching a flat or sharp, always move your hand *toward* the black key.

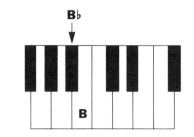

Each ♭ sign lasts a measure.

Two Excerpts from Symphony No. 1 by Brahms

1. Part of the fourth movement introduction.

The phrase mark indicates the musical sentence, but lift your hand briefly in measure 1 for the ⁊ rest.

Adapted from
Johannes Brahms (1833–1897)

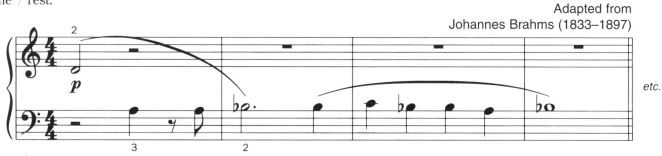

etc.

2. The first theme of the fourth movement.

(**E**♭ is the black key just to the left of **E.**)

etc.

Fascinating snippet

This symphony was not always well received. "Lovers of Brahms were much disturbed by large numbers of people leaving the hall between the movements of the *C Minor Symphony*....It must be admitted that to the larger part of our public, Brahms is still an incomprehensible terror." (*Evening Transcript*, Boston, 16 November 1885.)

Sharps

A **sharp** sign (♯) makes a note a one half-step *higher* (to the right on the keyboard);
e.g., F♯ is the black key just above **F.**

You will notice that most half steps
are from white to black keys or
black to white keys, but there are
also half steps between two sets of
white notes: **E - F** and **B - C.**

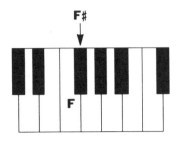

Each # sign lasts a measure.

Rigadoon

cresc. *(crescendo)* or ⟨ = gradually getting louder

dim. *(diminuendo)* or ⟩ = gradually getting softer

Adapted from
Henry Purcell (1659–1695)

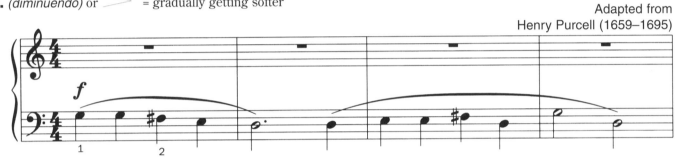

F♯ Workout!

Look carefully at the rests.

C.B.

23

Hands together

ALWAYS

- Practice hands separately at first and then, when each part is *perfect,* try the piece hands together *slowly.* Playing it faster is no problem once you know it well.
- Practice with the correct fingering.
- Practice beginning at any measure of the piece.
- Listen as you play.

Play these notes - *both hands* together.

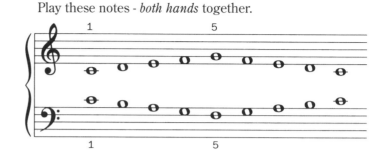

Hint

If the rhythms are very tricky, try tapping them out - tap out the R.H. rhythm on your right knee and the L.H. rhythm on your left knee. Practice knees separately, then knees together!

Three "Hands Together" Exercises

1. Follow the directions of the arrows - they have been added to this exercise to help you. Measures 1-2, hands move in similar motion (both hands moving together in the same direction). Measures 3-4, hands move in contrary motion (see page 14).

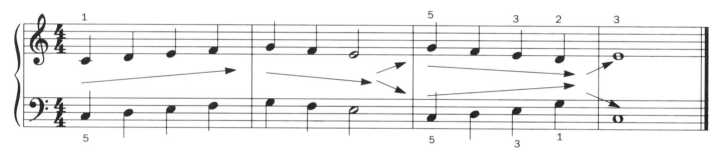

2. The beginning of an American Folk Song - "Old Woman."

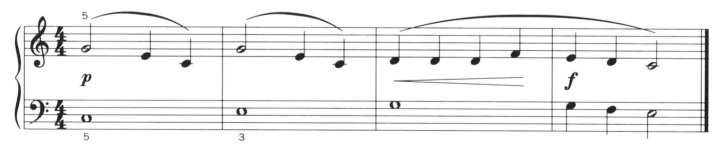

3. ! R.H. A hint of "Three Blind Mice."
L.H. A hint of "Frère Jacques."

24

First Study

HULTON DEUTSCH COLLECTION LIMITED

In the original version, the left hand plays chords. This simplified arrangement has been designed to develop coordination between the hands.

Adapted from
Karl Czerny (1791–1857)

Chords

Two or more notes played *together* are called a **chord.**

Find and play the chords below, saying both letter-names. (Use any suitable fingering.)

* If two notes of a chord are adjacent notes, the written notes fit sideways.

Drink to Me Only with Thine Eyes
An excerpt

In vocal music, singing more than one note on one syllable is shown by a slur; e.g., ♩♩♩ in measure 3 below.
with

Traditional English Song

Carefree John

Daniel Gottlieb Türk (1750–1813)

Reminder: Check that you are still holding your hands in a curved shape.

Miserable Mary!

C.B.

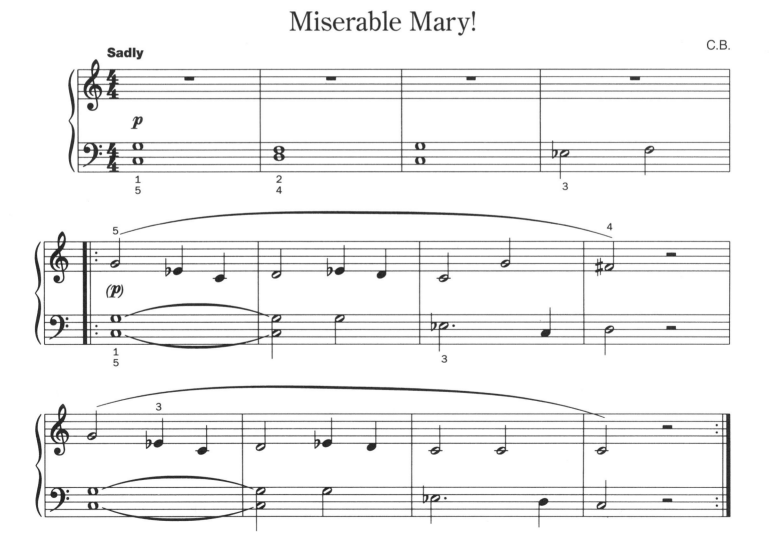

27

Expression marks

Composers use **expression marks** to make pieces sound more interesting and more musical. Most of these derive from Italian terms used since the Renaissance.

Dynamics

Notes can be varied by playing them with different degrees of weight and intensity.

Composers indicate their intentions by writing a dynamic marking under the note.

See page 11 for *f* and *p* and page 23 for *cresc.* and *dim.*

Here are some other common dynamics:

mf (mezzo forte) - moderately loud

mp (mezzo piano) - moderately soft

ff (fortissimo) - very loud

pp (pianissimo) - very soft

Tempo indications

At the beginning of most pieces you will find a word (or group of words) to show both the speed and the character of the music. They are not usually written in English as on page 27.

Here are a few of the most common ones:

Allegro = lively, quick (means "cheerful")   **Andante** = at a medium pace (walking speed)

Adagio = slow   **Largo** = very slow, stately   **Presto** = fast

Moderato = moderately (**Allegro moderato** = moderately fast)

Clog Dance

English Folk Dance

28

Gavotte

Ritardando
ritard.
rit.
} = getting gradually slower

poco = a little

a tempo = in time, indicating a return to the original speed after *rit.*

Ritenuto
riten.
rit.
} = slower, held back

poco rit. = slow down a little

Adapted from
James Hook (1746–1827)

New position

Place **both hands** in the position shown.

You are now ready to play the notes **G A B C D** in both hands - an octave apart.

Play these five notes in similar and contrary motion.

The **D** in the left hand is often called **Middle D** (see page 36).

A line over or under a note = a slight stress or pressure on the note.

Exercises

1.

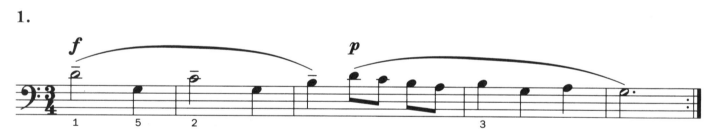

When you can play this exercise, try closing your eyes and playing it from memory.

Then play it with your *right hand,* starting on

2.

This is half of a tune you may recognize.

Play the repeated fourth-finger note quite firmly, but don't allow it to become "locked."

When you can play Exercise 2, close your eyes and play it from memory.

Then play it with the *left hand,* starting on

Der Meyen
"In the Month of May"

Swiss Folk Song

Teacher's accompaniment

31

Little Sonata
First movement*

Sometimes $\frac{4}{4}$ is written as **C** (common time).

Hint: Practice this piece hands separately and then together (see page 24).

Charles Henry Wilton (1761–1832)

* originally in another key.

Gavotte

The **Gavotte** is a dance originating from France.

It usually begins on the third beat of the measure, when the dancers traditionally raise their left feet.

Adapted from an excerpt by
George Frideric Handel (1685–1759)

Whole steps

A **whole step** is the distance of two half-steps; e.g., **C-D, F♯-G♯,** or **E-F♯.**

In **version 2** below, the gavotte you have just played is written out *one whole-step* lower.

{ R.H. *Change* your hand position, but the fingering remains as in **version 1.**

{ L.H. *Stay* in the same position as **version 1,** but start one finger lower.

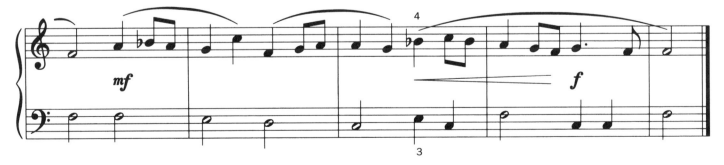

Rags

A piece of ragtime music is called a **rag.** Ragtime - an early jazz style - grew out of African-American music and was extremely popular as dance music around 1900.

Ragtime features syncopated rhythms; i.e., the musical accents occur on the weaker beats of the measure.

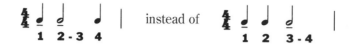

Tap out the rhythm of *Raccoon Rag* on your knees.

Raccoon Rag

Reminder: Each ♭ and ♯ sign lasts one measure and no longer; e.g., ordinary **B** in measure 7.

34

Naturals

A **natural** sign (♮) cancels a ♭ or a ♯ sign.

Sometimes you will see a ♮ sign in parentheses (♮). This isn't theoretically required, but acts as a helpful reminder that the note does not have a ♭ or a ♯ sign, although it is very near to one that has.

Exercise

Mopstick Rag

Fascinating snippet

Scott Joplin - the king of the piano rag - often wrote the following words above his music: "Notice! Don't play this piece fast. It is never right to play ragtime fast."

C.B.

More notes

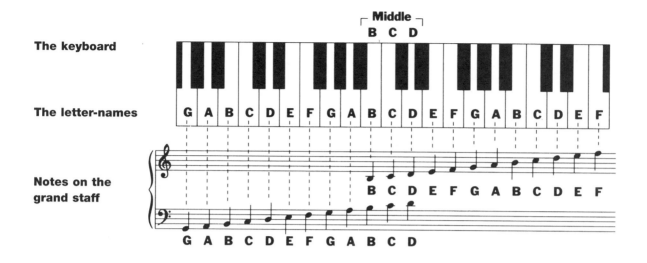

The keyboard

The letter-names

Notes on the grand staff

Different clef - Same notes

The two groups of notes below notate the same pitch. They are written here in both clefs so that either hand may play them.

Usually played with the left hand

Usually played with the right hand

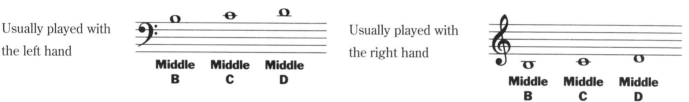

Middle B   Middle C   Middle D

Middle B   Middle C   Middle D

Note mnemonics

To help with the "geography" of the keyboard, you may find it useful to remember the letter-names of the notes on the lines and spaces by remembering certain sentences and words.

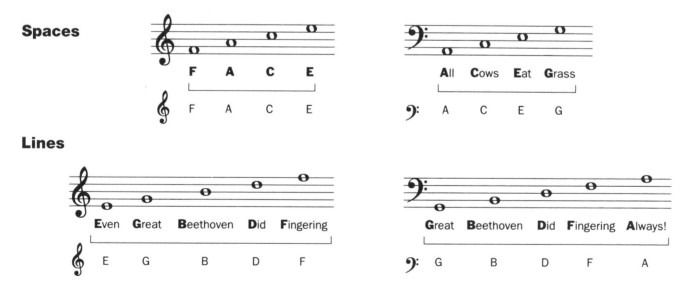

Spaces

F A C E

F A C E

All **Cows** **Eat** **Grass**

A C E G

Lines

Even **Great** **Beethoven** **Did** **Fingering**

E G B D F

Great **Beethoven** **Did** **Fingering** **Always!**

G B D F A

Sightreading (Playing at sight)

To become a good sightreader you need to develop the habit of reading notes as a pattern of shapes.

- Look at groups or phrases of notes.
- Observe whether they go up or down.
- Look at the pattern of each note group.

Reading note groups
Lines

Line notes

Moving line-to-line, you skip the space notes.

Play these four notes
with any finger.

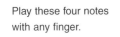

You will be skipping
these space notes.

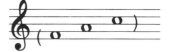

Note-finder exercises (line notes)

Find and play the following groups of notes. Say the letter-names as you play them.

Try not to look at your hands, however tempting!

On the Lines
(With a hint of Haydn!)*

*see page 14.

37

Reading note groups
Spaces

Space notes

Moving space-to-space, you skip the line notes.

Play these four notes with any finger.

You will be skipping these line notes.

Note-finder exercises (space notes)

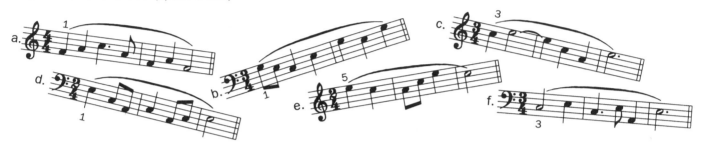

Spacial Concepts!

C.B.

In the style of a waltz

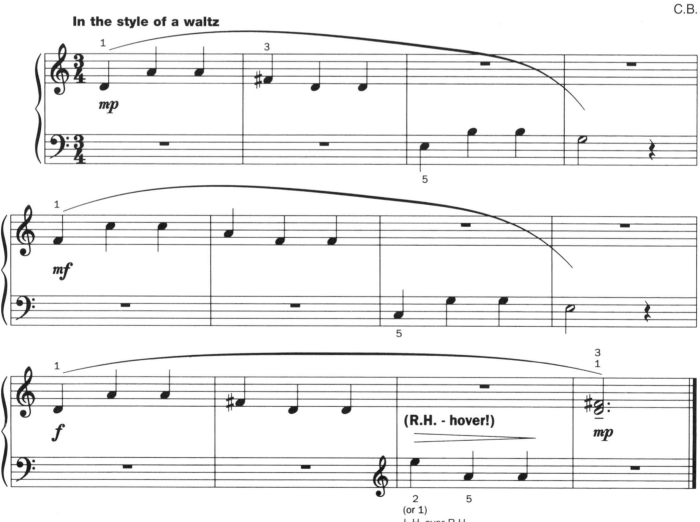

(R.H. - hover!)

2
(or 1)
L.H. over R.H.

38

Bobby Shaftoe

Traditional English Song

Move from phrase to phrase carefully, looking at each group of notes.

Teacher's accompaniment

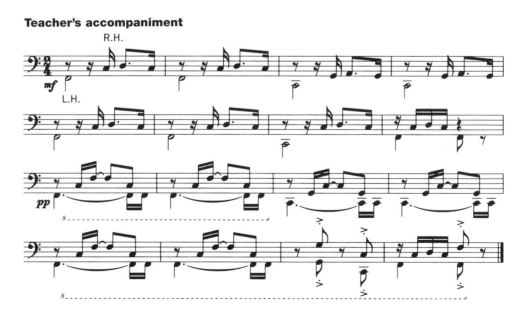

Two-Part Invention

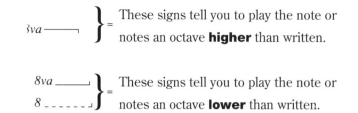

8va ⎤
⎱ = These signs tell you to play the note or
notes an octave **higher** than written.

8va ⎤
8 ⎱ = These signs tell you to play the note or
notes an octave **lower** than written.

C.B.

Suggested listening

J.S. Bach wrote a number of two- and three-part inventions
for his son Wilhelm Friedemann. Listen to these or Bach's
The Art of Fugue, written in the 1740s.

L'homme Armé

A traditional melody said to have been sung by the Crusaders (eleventh century).

Anonymous

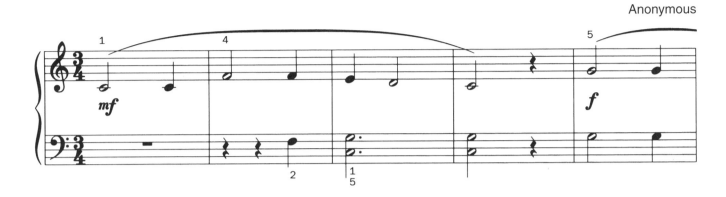

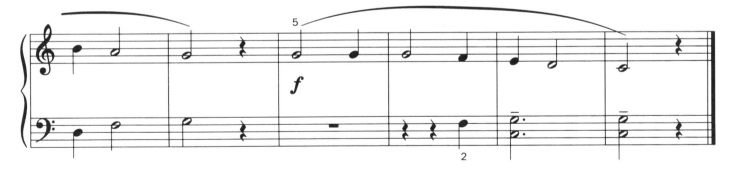

Fascinating snippet

The above song was passed by word of mouth from one generation to the next. The earliest printed music is said to be a book of plainsong issued in Southern Germany in 1473. It is a **Gradual** by an unknown composer.

Les Cinq Doigts

In this piece *both* hands play in the treble clef. In measure 13-14, 16-17, and 19-20, the note **G** is held with the left hand thumb for two beats, as fingers 2, 3, 4, and 5 play the ♫ ♫. This is called *part-playing;* i.e., two parts are played by one hand. Watch out for the time signature changes.

Moderato

Igor Stravinsky (1882–1971)

Fine

D.C. al Fine

Fascinating snippet

Igor Stravinsky, one of the greatest composers of the twentieth century, was known for his acerbic wit, as can be observed by the following quote: "Too many pieces finish too long after the end."

Key signatures

A **key signature,** when needed, is placed at the beginning of each line of music. It comes *after* the clef and *before* the time signature. The composer uses it as shorthand to avoid having to write in the relevant ♯s or ♭s each time.

All the **F**s will be
F♯ unless marked
with a ♮.

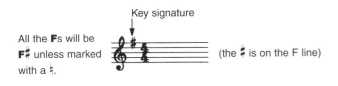

Key signature

(the ♯ is on the F line)

This is the key signature of G major* which has one sharp, F♯.

Russian Dance

Alexander Goedicke (1877–1957)

*The formation of major scales is explained in *Book 2*.

Monet's Garden
Secondo

Both hands are in the bass clef

The lines that are used above and below the staves are called *leger* lines. It's not worth changing clefs just for two notes.

Watch out for the time signature changes in this piece.

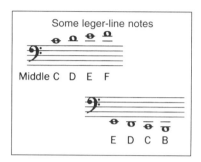

Some leger-line notes

Middle C   D   E   F

E   D   C   B

C.B.

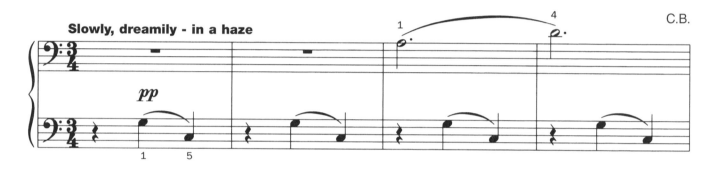

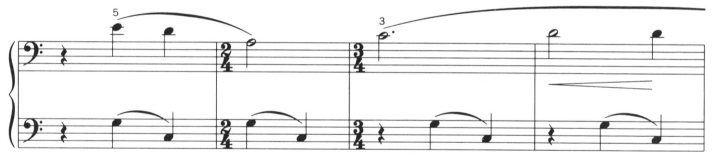

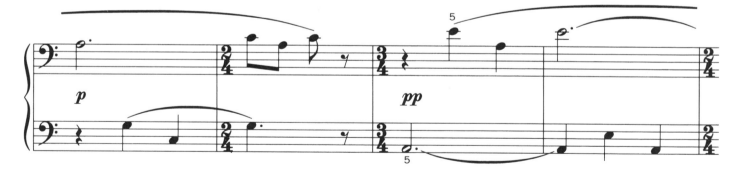

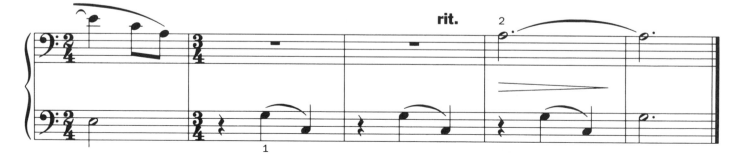

44

Duet

Monet's Garden
Primo
Both hands are in the treble clef

Press the pedal on the far right (the sustain pedal)
down with either foot for a special effect. Leave it
down throughout to give a blurred, impressionistic sound
to this duet. (This isn't the usual pedal technique!)

C.B.

45

Extending the hands

Prior to this page, the hands have usually played in five-note hand positions within each group or phrase:

From now on, the hands may be extending or contracting so that the range of notes within each phrase can be widened.

Exercises for the *Allemande* below:

1.   Hand extending   see measures 7 - 8 below.

2.   Hand contracting   see measures 9 - 10 below.

Allemande

Johann Hermann Schein (1586–1630)

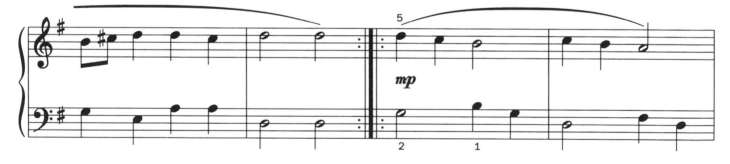

Another key signature

Key signature

(The ♭ is on the **B** line)

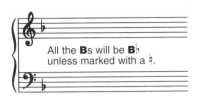

All the **B**s will be **B♭** unless marked with a ♮.

This is the key signature of F major, which has one flat, B♭

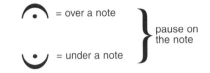

= over a note

= under a note

} pause on the note

Fingers-over-thumbs: another way to extend the hands.

(i)

see measures 6-7 below.

(ii)

Poor Wand'ring One
from *The Pirates of Penzance*

Adapted from
Arthur Sullivan (1842–1900)

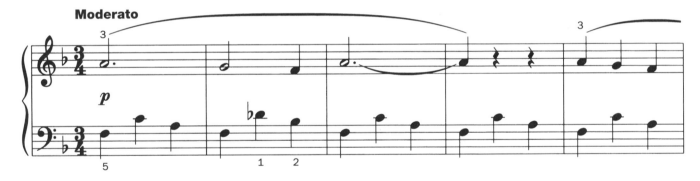

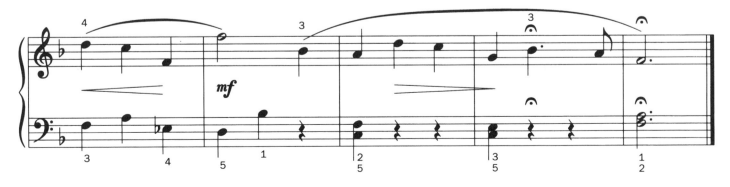

Scarborough Fair

Changing the fingering on one note.

This is a useful technique when running out of fingers.

(i) measures 6-7 L.H.

(ii) measures 10-11 R.H.

} practice these measures a few times.

Traditional English Song

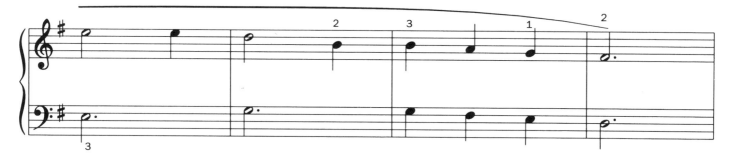

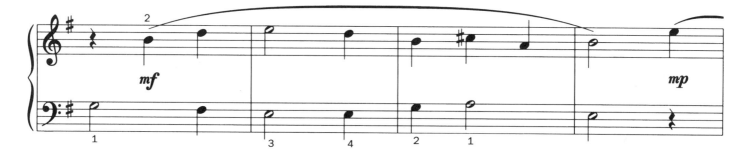

Suggested listening

Gaspard de la Nuit by Maurice Ravel (1875-1937) contains
some fiendishly difficult repeated notes.
Listen in awe!

Slurs

A **slur** is a curved line over or under a group of two or three notes:

Think of it as a very short phrase and float your hand from the keyboard between slurs. The weight is put on the first note of the slur and is released at the end of it.

Progress: Now that the pieces are gradually getting more difficult, don't expect instant achievement! Make sure that you practice hands separately until perfect before attempting hands together. Most of the pieces will take longer than a week to learn and it is worth spending time consolidating what you already know before moving on to a new topic.

Exercise

Now try it with the left hand starting an octave lower than written.

The note value of the last note of each slur will be reduced slightly; e.g., the first two bars should sound more like

Cradle Song

Dmitri Kabalevsky (1904–1987)

German Dance

First and second endings.

The end of a section of music that is repeated can be altered when it is played the second time by the use of **1.** **2.** directions. Don't forget to leave out the **1.** measure (or passage) when you play the second ending.

Adapted from
Franz Schubert (1797–1828)

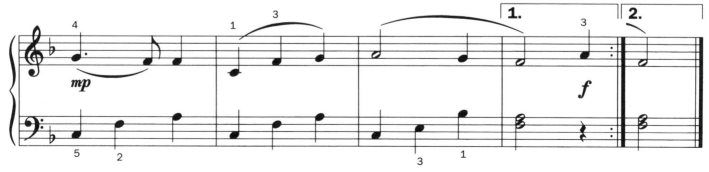

Don Giovanni
Zerlina's aria *"Batti, batti, o bel Masetto"*
"Do not spare me, dear Masetto"

Adapted from
Wolfgang Amadeus Mozart (1756–1791)

Fascinating snippet

This opera was a great success in Prague, but a failure in Vienna.
Emperor Joseph pronounced it "heavenly," but felt that is was "no food
for the teeth of my Viennese." This was the same emperor who
declared that Mozart's music had "too many notes," to which Mozart
replied, "Just as many as are needed, your Majesty."

Staccato

Staccato is an Italian word meaning "disconnected" or "detached." It is the opposite of *legato*. This touch is indicated by a dot over or under a note:

Release the piano key, as soon as you hear the sound, by a quick upward motion of the hand. Make sure that your fingers are bent and that your wrist is loose, thereby allowing your hand to spring back after each note. You are aiming to produce short, crisp notes. (In the eighteenth century the staccato touch was not so crisp and was only *slightly* detached.)

Staccato exercises

1.

2.

Fascinating snippet

During World War II, the opening bars of Beethoven's *Fifth Symphony* took on an important significance. The four-note theme played dot-dot-dot-dash (dot = staccato; dash = stress) was found to represent the letter *V* in Morse Code. As well as this coincidence, this is the *Fifth Symphony* - Roman Numeral V. This work came to represent the "V for Victory" slogan.

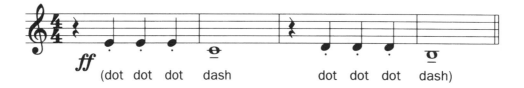

(dot dot dot   dash   dot dot dot   dash)

Staccato Study

Make sure that the notes of both hands sound exactly together. Keep the wrist loose but don't allow the repeated staccato notes to get "flabby" or lazy.

Karl Czerny (1791–1857)

If you are in a group situation, this study sounds really impressive when played on more than one keyboard, or with several players at one keyboard, each playing one hand using all the available octaves.

La Traviata
Drinking song *Libiamo* from Act I
"Let's drink"

The left-hand chord-notes in parentheses are actually
needed (and played) by the right-hand tune. You can
either omit them in the left hand or play the **D** in
both hands.

Adapted from
Giuseppe Verdi (1813–1901)

Air in F

Dots inside a slur  indicate *semi-staccato* (half-staccato). The notes should be played slightly separated but not as much as staccato. This kind of touch is used for most of the music of the Baroque era—e.g., J.S. Bach, Handel, and Purcell—when played on the piano rather than a harpsichord.

Attributed to
Johann Sebastian Bach (1685–1750)

Fascinating snippet

This piece is from the *Anna Magdalena Bach Notenbüchlein* of 1725, which Bach compiled for his second wife. Many of the pieces were untitled so we can't be sure which ones Bach wrote himself.

The sustain pedal
Sometimes called the *damper* pedal

Most pianos have two or three pedals, but to start with use only the one on the right - the **sustain pedal** (sometimes incorrectly called the "loud pedal"). When this pedal is pressed down, the dampers are lifted from the strings, allowing the strings to vibrate without restriction and thereby giving a fuller and more enriched sound.

Place the ball of your right foot on this pedal and rest your heel on the floor. Now press the pedal down several times as quietly as possible, keeping your heel on the floor. Keep the sole of your foot in contact with the pedal all the time you use it - the ankle should feel like a hinge.

Reasons for using this pedal:

1. To sustain and join sounds that cannot be played legato by the hands (usually notes belonging to the same chord but which are out of reach).
2. To connect different chords and make them legato - this overlapping is often called *legato pedaling*.

There are several markings to indicate the pedal, but the following one is the most common nowadays:

The pedal is pressed down at the beginning and released immediately at the end of the sign.

1. Try playing the following exercises without the pedal to start with, so that you can hear the difference it makes to the sound.

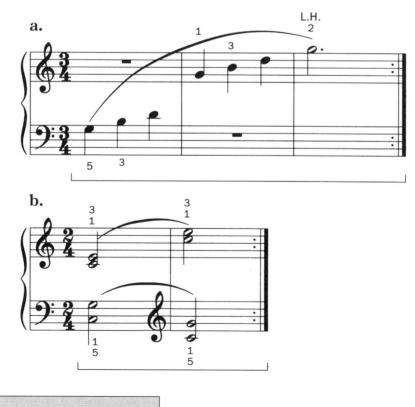

Fascinating snippet
Chopin called the sustain pedal "the soul of the piano."

2. In the exercise below, connect one note to the next by letting the pedal come up just at the moment when the key is played, and then pressing the pedal down again before the finger leaves the key.

The fingering below will make it impossible to play legato without the use of the pedal. The counts are given to make it easier for you to see and feel where to change the pedal and the ——∧—— marking has therefore been exaggerated.

a. D = down   U = up

Legato pedaling allows the next note or chord to be "trapped" and sustained.

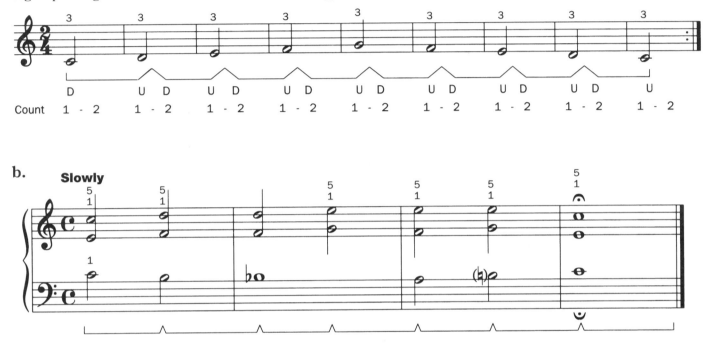

b.

c.

Legato pedaling is used here in the eight measures of *The Beautiful Blue Danube* below. If the pedal was left down for three measures, the effect would be too heavy for the staccato chords in the right hand.

Johann Strauss II (1825–1899)

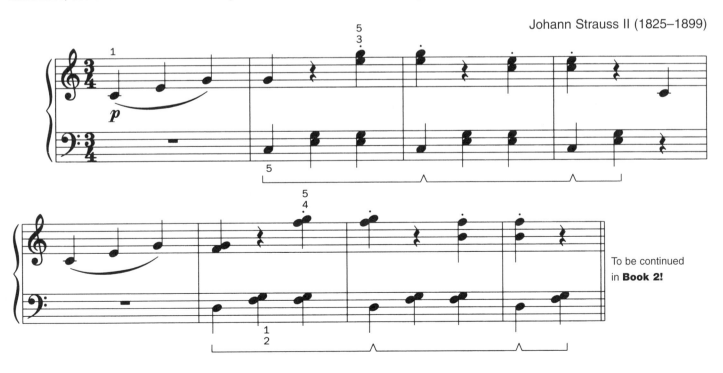

To be continued in **Book 2!**

57

Valse

MARY EVANS PICTURE LIBRARY

Before playing a new piece with the pedal, always practice it *without* at first. You may not want to use the pedal with every piece.

Here the tune is in the left hand, so try to bring it out.

Adapted from
Frédéric Chopin (1810–1849)

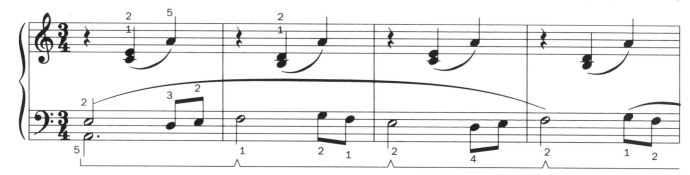

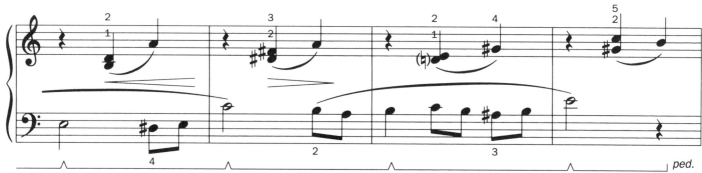

ped.
sim.

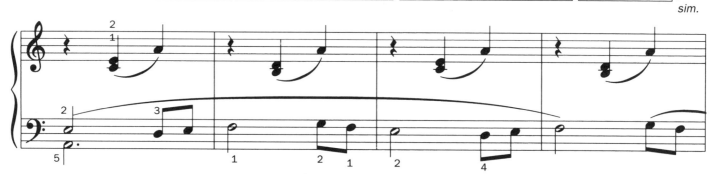

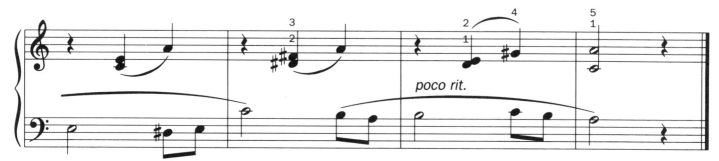

poco rit.

Suggested listening

Famous waltzes to listen to are: Op.18 in E-flat; Op. 34, No.1 in A-flat; Op. 64, No.1 in D-flat (the "Minute Waltz"); and Op. 34, No. 2 in A minor.

Lullaby

Adapted from
Johannes Brahms (1833–1897)

Fascinating snippet

"I have played over the music of that scoundrel Brahms. What a
giftless bastard." - Tchaikovsky, 1886.

Auld Lang Syne

You may be called upon to play this on New Year's Eve!

Scottish

Theme from
Swan Lake

In most music, pedal markings are not written in.

Try changing the pedal where you think suitable and where the notes of the chord change.

Experiment with the sounds you want.

Adapted from
Peter Ilyich Tchaikovsky (1840–1893)

Für Elise

Adapted from an excerpt by
Ludwig van Beethoven (1770–1827)

Andante con moto*

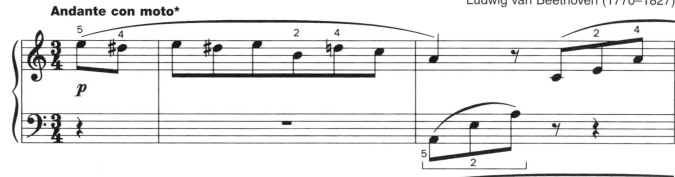

* see page 64 for **con moto**

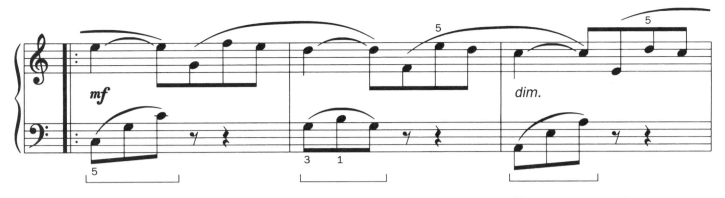

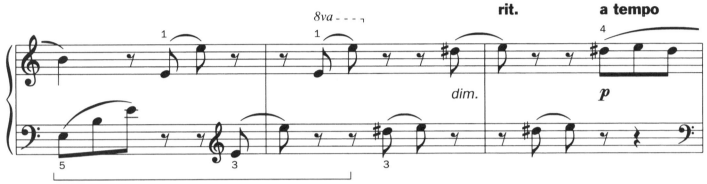

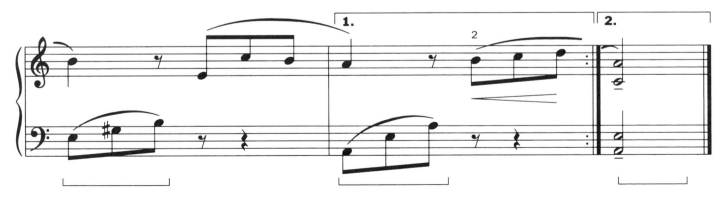

Dictionary of terms
used in Book 1

ff (fortissimo) =very loud

pp (pianissimo) =very soft

f (forte) loud

p (piano) soft

mf (mezzo forte) moderately loud

mp (mezzo piano) moderately soft

cresc. (crescendo) or ⟨ = gradually getting louder

dim. (diminuendo) or ⟩ = gradually getting softer

Presto = fast

Allegro = lively, quick (means "cheerful")

Moderato = moderately (**Allegro moderato** = moderately fast)

Allegretto = fairly quick but not as quick as **Allegro**

Andante = at a medium pace (walking speed)

Andantino = an ambiguous term! It can mean slightly faster or slightly slower than **Andante**

Adagio = slow

Lento = slow

Largo = very slow, stately

Andante con moto = at a medium pace but with movement
(***con*** = with, ***moto*** = movement)

Ritardando
ritard.
rit.
} = getting gradually slower

Ritenuto
riten.
rit.
} = getting slower, held back

poco = a little

poco rit. = slow down a little

a tempo = in time, indicating a return to the original speed
after: **rit.**

grazioso = gracefully

espressivo = expressively

con brio = with spirit

simile = same as previously indicated

:| = Repeat sign = repeat from the beginning or from the nearest |:

D.C. (*Da Capo*) = repeat from the beginning

D.C. al Fine = go back to the beginning and finish at the word
Fine

Well done!

You are now ready for **Book 2.** This contains many favorites including "The Entertainer" by Scott Joplin (used in the film *The Sting*), "Can-Can" by Offenbach, "The Beautiful Blue Danube" by Johann Strauss II, and many more.
Topics include major scales,

You are also ready to play:
A Feast of Easy Carols by Carol Barratt
A Second Feast of Easy Carols by Carol Barratt

Look out for supplementary material in the forthcoming series: *The Classic Piano Collection* by Carol Barratt.

Keep practicing!

Carol Barratt